JUST
· WRITE ·
ONE THING
· TODAY ·

METRO BOOKS
New York

An Imprint of Sterling Publishing Co., Inc.
1166 Avenue of the Americas
New York, NY 10036

ISBN 978-1-4351-6559-5

For information about custom editions, special sales, and premium and corporate
purchases, please contact Sterling Special Sales at 800-805-5489
or specialsales@sterlingpublishing.com.

Manufactured in China

4 6 8 10 9 7 5 3

www.sterlingpublishing.com

JUST
·WRITE·
ONE THING
·TODAY·

365 Creative Prompts
to Inspire You Every Day

John Gillard

METRO BOOKS
New York

HOW THE BOOK WORKS

Each page of the book is color coded with one of four different color tabs. This indicates the type of writing prompt for each day.

SINGLE-PAGE PROMPTS

Longer exercises, allowing a flow of writing and development of key writing skills such as tone, setting, characterization, and dialogue.

FIRST HALF-PAGE PROMPTS

Shorter exercises developing concise, textured descriptions, different ways of looking at the world around us, and clever wordplay.

SECOND HALF-PAGE PROMPTS

Promoting the same key elements of writing as the upper half-page prompts and often following on from the previous day's prompt.

INTENSIVE WEEK

More intensive writing exercises, which require your own larger notepad in order to write a longer piece. Intensive weeks promote plot progression, pace, narrative style, characterization, richness of language, and more.

INTRODUCTION

Just Write One Thing Today offers inspiration and prompts to help you write each and every day, enjoying all the pleasures and benefits that daily writing brings.

You can use this book to stretch your writing muscles and kick-start a morning, afternoon, or day of writing, while enhancing your literary skills. Putting pen to paper every day can help you build a picture of common ideas, themes, and tones within your writing. These might inform a longer piece of work, or simply get the creative juices flowing for the day.

Douglas Coupland, who wrote *Generation X*, once said, "If we were to collect these small moments in a notebook and save them over a period of months we would see certain trends emerge from our collection—certain voices would emerge that have been trying to speak through us." In fact, it was the daily notes he made over a year that formed the ideas and content for his acclaimed compilation of vignettes, *Waiting For God*. The classic British novelist Virginia Woolf kept a writing journal in order to write each and every day. *Just Write* invites you to do the very same.

Get your pen flowing across the page. Don't worry too much about punctuation and grammar. Take as much or as little time as you like or can afford to each day. This book is there for you to enjoy your writing and to get your writing muscles flexing daily, whether taking them for a gentle stretch, a longer walk, or even a speedy sprint.

> "Keep a small can of WD-40 on your desk—away from any open flames—to remind yourself that if you don't write daily, you will get rusty."
> —George Singleton

1

TURMERIC-YELLOW TAXIS

Write down the colors of various herbs and spices and then use these spice/color couplets to describe the color of something else, such as "turmeric-yellow New York taxis."

HISTORICAL JUXTAPOSITION

In the space below each of these three historical events, describe a seemingly mundane, everyday event that might have occurred on the same day, which serves to juxtapose the famous events:

William Shakespeare dies, April 23, 1616

The California Gold Rush begins, January 24, 1848

Tim Berners-Lee releases the World Wide Web: the Internet goes live to the world, August 6, 1991

JESUS WEPT

"Jesus wept" is the shortest sentence in the Bible, made up of only a noun and a verb. List random nouns and verbs below and see if any fit well together to create a short, impactful, and perfectly crafted sentence:

Noun   **Verb**

e.g. windmills   sing

4 BIRD THOUGHTS

Think of a specific type of bird, such as a wandering albatross, and write a detailed description of it, including its appearance and its movements, and perhaps even its thoughts.

5 EXPANDING NOUNS

Write a short passage describing a walk around an antique shop, museum, or old period house. Once you have finished, pick out four or five nouns and verbs and replace them with words that have an alternative meaning but which read cohesively, to create something new and potentially unexpected: "We walked to the reception" might become "We triumphed to the reception."

6 TEXTURE

Add a layer or two of detail to the items listed below to add texture. For example, a "sword" becomes a "16th-century Samurai sword."

- gloves
- truck
- briefcase

7 MASTERPIECES

"The family is one of nature's masterpieces."
—George Santayana

Write down some things you consider to be examples of "life's masterpieces."

INTENSIVE WEEK

Get your notebook and prepare to write five longer pieces.

8   **REACHING THE SUMMIT:** Write a short monologue (internal thoughts and musings) from the perspective of a mountaineer who has just reached the summit after a long and treacherous climb and can see for miles around. They could describe the scene, the experience, and how they feel, or they could simply muse as they look over the world.

9   **THE WOODEN BENCH:** Write dialogue between two people who are walking up a path in the country toward a solitary wooden bench, which sits at the top of the hill.

10   **STREAM OF CONSCIOUSNESS:** Write the inner thoughts of a washed-up entertainer who has had his or her fifteen minutes of fame but now performs in rundown clubs, spending most of the time at the bar drinking Scotch. Write in stream of consciousness, a free-flowing style with each thought running continuously on from the last. Try to put yourself fully into the mind of the character and let your pen glide across the page.

11   **ECLECTIC SETTINGS:** Write a short story based in one or all of the following settings: a casino, a pool hall, a disused subway station, a Turkish bath.

12   **LOST:** Write about a time when you were lost, in whatever form that might be, real or metaphorical. Or write about an imagined person who has lost their way.

> "I have always been delighted at the prospect of a new day, a fresh try, one more start, with perhaps a bit of magic waiting somewhere behind the morning."
> —J. B. Priestley

13 OLD SHOES

Describe a pair of old shoes that have just been found in the attic or basement.

_____

_____

_____

_____

_____

_____

_____

_____

_____

14 BACK STORY

What is the back story of yesterday's shoes? Who did they belong to?

_____

_____

_____

_____

_____

_____

_____

_____

_____

STUCK IN THE CARPOOL LANE

"We're past the age of heroes and hero kings . . . Most of our lives are basically mundane and dull, and it's up to the writer to find ways to make them interesting."
—John Updike

Take these mundane chores and add something to each sentence, which might serve to spice it up and make it interesting.

I put the washing machine on a full cycle . . .

_____

_____

_____

We were stuck in the carpool lane on the way to the office . . .

_____

_____

_____

She ordered bacon, eggs, some toast on the side, and a long black . . .

_____

_____

_____

The line for passport control was long and very, very slow . . .

_____

_____

_____

WINTERTIME

Write about a vivid wintertime memory. Perhaps you remember a special time playing in the snow?

17

FLAVORS

Write down five of your favorite drinks. Describe in detail the enjoyment you feel when drinking them. The flavors, the layers of taste, the memories they conjure up.

_____

_____

_____

_____

_____

_____

_____

_____

_____

_____

_____

_____

_____

_____

_____

_____

_____

_____

_____

_____

_____

_____

_____

A FLAME

Describe a flame from a burning candle, a fire, or a lighter. Our minds inevitably wander when we look into a flame. Write down your fire-inspired musings or those of an imagined character.

SLICED BREAD

Change one or two words from each of the following clichés to make new, more unexpected phrases.

The best thing since sliced bread

The best thing since . . .

_____

_____

_____

Two heads are better than one

Two . . . are better than one

_____

_____

If you can't stand the heat, get out of the kitchen

If you can't stand the . . . get out of the . . .

_____

_____

_____

The answer can be found at the bottom of a glass

The answer can be found at . . .

_____

_____

_____

20 THE WEIRD AND THE WONDERFUL

Below are some weird and wonderful book titles. Using these
as inspiration, write down three potential titles for short stories,
novels, poems, or whatever it is you may want to write.

- *How to Disappear Completely and Never Be Found,* by Doug Richmond
- *How to Avoid Huge Ships,* by Captain John W. Trimmer
- *Stray Shopping Carts of Eastern North America,* by Julian Montague

----

----

21 LOVE AND HATE

Write down ten words or sentences to describe, or that you
associate with, love and hate.

INTENSIVE WEEK

Get your notebook and prepare to write five longer pieces.

22

CHARACTER PROFILE: Write a profile for an invented character. This can be a paragraph, writing about what makes them tick, their back story (perhaps they have a terrible secret or traumatic past), any unique individual traits, their job, what they love, what they hate, their strengths, and their weaknesses. Or you could write a list, including:

- Physical description
- Personality traits
- Mannerisms and quirks
- Goals
- Conflicts
- Relationships

23

INNER CONFLICT: Write a monologue from the perspective of somebody who is a part of a warring family and is experiencing some kind of inner conflict.

24

GOLD RUSH: Describe the scene of a Gold-Rush town, either in its heyday or as a ghost town as it is today.

25

ROAD SWEEPER: Write about the city of Rio de Janeiro, or another city of your choice, from an unusual perspective, such as from the point of view of a road sweeper.

26

TEN-MINUTE FLOW: Write continuously for ten minutes or longer, using the title *After the Chill* as an initial spark. Let your thoughts flow from one to the next without much, if any, deliberation. Do not worry too much about spelling and grammar; the key is to stretch your writing muscles and see where your thoughts take you.

> *"Exercise the writing muscle every day, even if it is only a letter, notes, a title list, a character sketch, a journal entry. Writers are like dancers, like athletes. Without that exercise, the muscles seize up."*
>
> —Jane Yolen

27 BETTER WHEN OLD

"Age appears to be best in four things; old wood best to burn, old wine to drink, old friends to trust, and old authors to read."
—Francis Bacon

Write down three or four other things that are better when old.

_____

_____

_____

_____

_____

_____

_____

_____

28 WEDDING DAYS

Write down ten words you associate with wedding days.

_____

_____

_____

_____

_____

_____

_____

_____

_____

29 BLACK LEATHER JACKET

Think of objects that might be made of the following natural materials and describe them in detail, perhaps also putting them into a context. For example, "The once black leather jacket was now a rough, mottled gray like Venetian marble jarring wonderfully with the stark red stitched writing on the back, 'Hell's Angels MC Berdoo.'"

- leather
- wood
- coal
- cotton

_____

_____

_____

_____

_____

_____

_____

_____

_____

_____

_____

_____

_____

_____

_____

_____

_____

_____

30 WHAT'S IN A TITLE?

Write down words you associate with the following book, movie, and song titles:

- *To Kill a Mockingbird*, by Harper Lee
- *The Shawshank Redemption*
- "Wichita Lineman," by Jimmy Webb

31 WEATHER WORDS

Write down ten words associated with different kinds of weather.

32 WASHED ASHORE

Write down five objects that might be found washed up on the seashore.

----

33 FOUND OBJECTS

Expand upon yesterday's found objects, describing them in detail.

----

34 LINCOLN'S TOP HAT

Write a description of three famous historical characters using their clothes to represent their character. For example, "Abraham Lincoln's magnificent, tall, straight-edged top hat."

35 DENTIST PARTNER

Using the book titles below for inspiration, write internal dialogue of a character contemplating their dentist husband or wife:

- *How to Live with an Idiot,* by John Hoover
- *Managing a Dental Practice: The Genghis Khan Way,* by Michael Young
- *Highlights in the History of Concrete,* by Christopher C. Stanley

INTENSIVE WEEK

Get your notebook and prepare to write five longer pieces.

36 **PRISON POINTS OF VIEW:** A riot has broken out in a maximum-security prison. Write three short passages, either in the first person ("I") or the third person ("he/she/they"), showing the action from the point of view of:
- one of the guards trying to control the riot
- one of the central instigators
- an inmate who is close to parole and trying desperately not to become embroiled

37 **TITLE:** *Into the Dark*
Write a short story, dialogue, monologue, scene, poem, or any other form you are inspired to employ, using the title above.

38 **GRAVE CONSEQUENCES:** Write a scene in which a small group of people make a discovery that will have grave consequences either for themselves, their community, or the world. Ensure the action and dialogue does not get confused by organizing the roles and hierarchy of the characters before you start writing.

39 **CAVEMAN:** Explain to a caveman the ways in which the world will evolve from their time to the present day.

40 **GRYTVIKEN:** Write a scene or short story set in the Antarctic, where the ice has melted away, revealing something unexpected in the abandoned whaling station at Grytviken.

> "A story is a letter that the author writes to himself, to tell himself things that he would be unable to discover otherwise."
> —Carlos Ruiz Zafón

41 A CORAL REEF

Imagine swimming underwater around a coral reef. Describe what you feel and what you see.

----

42 SURROUNDINGS

Write a description of your current surroundings.

AUTHOR SIMILES

Create your own similes in place of the authors' similes below.

" . . . utterly absorbed by the curious experience that still clung to him like a garment."—*Magnificent Obsession*, by Lloyd C. Douglas

. . . utterly absorbed by the curious experience that still clung to him like . . .

_____

_____

_____

"Past him, ten feet from his front wheels, flung the Seattle Express like a flying volcano."—*Arrowsmith*, by Sinclair Lewis

Past him, ten feet from his front wheels, flung the Seattle Express like . . .

_____

_____

_____

"The very mystery of him excited her curiosity like a door that had neither lock nor key."—*Gone with the Wind*, by Margaret Mitchell

The very mystery of him excited her curiosity like . . .

_____

_____

_____

"The late afternoon sky bloomed in the window for a moment like the blue honey of the Mediterranean."—*The Great Gatsby*, by F. Scott Fitzgerald

The late afternoon sky bloomed in the window for a moment like . . .

_____

_____

_____

CHARACTER PAINTING: LANDSCAPE

Think of, or find an image of, a famous landscape painting. Write down what you or an imagined character might be thinking if the scene were real and you, or they, were standing within it.

45

SPRINGTIME

Write about a vivid springtime memory or description of springtime, when leaves are forming on the trees and the days are getting longer.

EVERYDAY OBJECTS

Write an unusual, unexpected description of the following everyday objects:

- laptop
- toaster
- notebook
- wallet
- flower pot
- hammer

OUTSIDE INSPIRATION

Look outside, or if you are outside look around you, and find an object, such as a piece of litter or a park bench. Describe the object and continue to write, letting your mind take you in any direction, without stopping, until you reach the end of the page.

48 SPOONERISMS

Dr. Spooner was a long-serving Oxford University Don, known for his accidental humorous turns of phrase. He would mix up the first letters of words within a sentence, for example:
"A blushing crow" (a crushing blow)
"A well-boiled icicle" (well-oiled bicycle)

Can you come up with any spoonerisms of your own?

----

49 SPOONERISMS, PART TWO

Use yesterday's spoonerisms, either your own or the examples given, within a paragraph or piece of dialogue.

INTENSIVE WEEK

Get your notebook and prepare to write five longer pieces.

50   **LIGHT RELIEF:** Create a character profile of a person who might bring light relief and humor to a story.

51   **TEN-MINUTE FLOW:** Using the title *The Wait is Over* to spark your imagination, write continuously for ten minutes or longer. Allow your thoughts to run on from one to the next, without too much consideration for spelling and grammar. The aim is to write freely and instinctively.

52   **RUNDOWN MOTEL:** Set the scene for some action to unfold within an old rundown motel.

53   **A COLORFUL CHAT:** "It ain't whatcha write, it's the way atcha write it." —Jack Kerouac

Write some dialogue between two people having a general chat about anything, however interesting, profound, or mundane, breaking up the language in a similar vein to the Kerouac quotation above to give them an interesting tone of voice.

54   **TITLE:** *Stolen Identity*
Finding inspiration from the title above, write a short story, dialogue, monologue, scene, poem, or whichever form you wish.

> "The greatest good you can do for another is not just share your riches, but to reveal to him his own."
>
> —Benjamin Disraeli

55 MELLOW

Use the adjectives below to create descriptions of people, places, or things:

- mellow
- soft
- mild
- natural
- delicate
- gentle

_____

_____

_____

_____

_____

_____

_____

56 TIME PORTAL

You, or an imagined character, are in the year AD 2200. Where are you, how did you get there, and what do you see?

_____

_____

_____

_____

_____

_____

_____

_____

IN THE NICK OF TIME

Reframe the following clichés to make a phrase that is less obvious, more interesting, and more dynamic, but which offers the same meaning:

In the nick of time (to happen just in time)

As brave as a lion (a very brave person)

Frightened to death (to be too frightened)

At the speed of light (to do something very quickly)

OBJECTS IN THE CLOSET

Look inside a drawer or in a closet and take out an object that you find there. Describe the object and continue to write, letting your mind take you in any direction, without stopping, until you reach the end of the page.

BIRD COLORS

Write down the colors of various birds and animals and then use these animal/color couplets to describe the color of something else, such as "flamingo-pink bubblegum."

WORD CONSTRAINT: BOOKS

Pick three of your favorite book titles. Count the number of letters in the title and write a short description or review of the book using this number of words.

e.g. *The Curious Case of Benjamin Button* = 30 letters
Description/review = 30 words

"If I waited for perfection . . . I would never write a word."

—Margaret Atwood

THIS PLACE

Starting with the sentence "I had never seen anywhere like this place before . . ." write continuously, without stopping, until you reach the end of the page.

62 AN EPIPHANY

An imagined character, who works in a job they have no passion for, in a run-down office block, has an epiphany. They have decided to do something completely different with their lives. Write about what it is they are going to do.

63 TEXTURE

Add a layer or two of detail to the things listed below to add texture. For example, "coffee beans" become "ground Ethiopian coffee beans."

- machete
- newspaper
- paperweight
- revolver

INTENSIVE WEEK

Get your notebook and prepare to write five longer pieces.

64

TITLE: *Stolen Identity*
Using the title above, write a short story, dialogue, monologue, scene, poem, or whatever form you are inspired to write.

65

PLOT OUTLINE: Draw up a potential plot outline for a story. Think of a character who has a specific goal that they are at present unable to reach. Ask yourself, and try to come up with answers to, the questions: What makes the main protagonist tick? Who or what is stopping them from reaching their goal? Who or what is helping them? How might they overcome these hurdles? (This will drive the story.) What is the setting? Do any specific scenes and characters begin to emerge? You will find a vivid and workable plot start to appear.

66

THE ELEVATOR: You're stuck in an elevator with four other people. Who are they (real, imagined, or famous)? After an hour, where has conversation led?

67

DIALOGUE INTERCHANGE AND PACE: Write internal dialogue from the perspective of a couple trying to rescue their marriage. Alternate from one to the other throughout the piece to create a dynamic interchange.

68

PICKPOCKET: Write about a day in the life of a pickpocket.

> "Be courageous and try to write in a way that scares you a little."
>
> —Holly Gerth

69 AN OLD WATCH

Describe an old watch that has been found covered in cobwebs in a box in the attic.

----

70 AN ANGRY EXCHANGE

Write a short exchange between an angry customer returning faulty or damaged goods to a shop.

UNEXPECTED COMPARISONS

Take these common similes and make up new, unexpected comparisons:

As busy as a bee

As busy as a . . .

_____

_____

_____

As strong as an ox

As strong as an . . .

_____

_____

_____

_____

As clean as a whistle

As clean as a . . .

_____

_____

_____

As light as a feather

As light as . . .

_____

_____

_____

_____

72 AUTOMOBILE REPAIR SHOP

Write down all the sounds and smells you might experience in an automobile repair shop or gas station.

---

73 OUTSIDE THE WINDOW

Look outside your window or, if you are outside, look at what is in front of you. Write what you see, paying close attention to the detail.

---

74 REFLECTIONS

Imagine either yourself or a fictitious character looking at a reflection, whether it be in a mirror, a pond, a shop window, or something else, and describe what is seen along with any evoked feelings.

75 REFLECTIONS, PART TWO

Write a reflection on a time gone by, a specific incident in the past, or life in general, either from your own perspective or that of an imagined character.

76 DETECTIVES

Write down ten words or phrases you associate with police detectives.

77 DETECTIVES, PART TWO

Write a paragraph about police detectives using none of yesterday's words.

INTENSIVE WEEK

Get your notebook and prepare to write five longer pieces.

78 **A BUILDING THAT SPEAKS**: Write a short piece from the perspective of a building (e.g. a house, a barn, or a museum) describing the world surrounding it, memories of events that have graced the building, or anything that only the walls of the building might know.

79 **TEN-MINUTE FLOW**: In order to stretch your writing muscles and see where your thoughts lead you, write without pause for ten minutes or longer, using the title *Falling in Silence* as a starting point.

80 **THE MAP**: "What if . . .?" scenarios, whereby an imagined scenario is posed as a speculative question, can be used for ideas generation and plot development. Write a short story, scene, or plot outline using the "What if . . .?" scenario below:

What if you were left a map, with detailed coordinates scribbled upon it, in the will of somebody you never knew?

81 **WIGWAM**: Describe the scene within a wigwam, either when used by Native American families to live in or for modern ceremonial occasions.

82 **CASTLE**: Write a short story, scene, or passage that includes a castle.

> *"The most beautiful things are those that madness prompts and reason writes."*
> —*André Gide*

83 ACRONYMS

Try to come up with acronyms for existing words, which relate directly to that word. The meaning may have a fictitious context. For example, "h.o.m.e" stands for "his onerous mother's empire."

----

84 TEXTURES

Write five words used to describe textures of objects and materials. Match each texture word with a human attribute. For example, "grainy voice."

Texture   **Human attribute**

TORNADOES

Use similes to describe and expand upon the effects of the extreme weather conditions below. For instance, "Tornadoes suck up garden gates and fences into the sky, tossing them about like socks in the tumble drier."

- tornadoes
- monsoons
- tidal waves/mega tsunamis

SPEED

Write about things that travel at great speed, such as a bullet, a sneeze, a leopard, or a Formula One car.

87 AN EARLY MEMORY

Write about a very early memory. Do you have a clear first memory?

A MOUNTAINOUS LANDSCAPE

You're on a bicycle traveling slowly across a mountainous landscape. Describe what you see and how you feel.

CITIES OF THE WORLD

What word, words, or sentences come to mind when you think
about the following cities? If any city is unknown to you, make it up.

Geneva (Switzerland)

Bógota (Colombia)

Beijing (China)

Sydney (Australia)

90 AN ANCIENT VASE

Describe an ancient ceramic vase.

91 UNEXPECTED ASSOCIATIONS

Describe various people of different character and age using descriptions/names of trees to create unexpected associations. For example, "Elderly men basking in the sun like majestic Madagascan baobab trees."

INTENSIVE WEEK

Get your notebook and prepare to write five longer pieces.

92 **THE DAWN CHORUS**: Describe the sounds of the following:
- the dawn chorus (early morning birdsong)
- a flag flapping in the wind
- a sheet of paper being ripped
- the tapping of keys on a computer
- a large number of coins being dropped on the floor

93 **TITLE**: *The Calm Before Tomorrow*
Using the title above as inspiration, create a short piece of writing in the form of your choosing.

94 **TIME CAPSULE, 1897**: A time capsule has been found following the digging up of ground in a public park. It is discovered that the capsule was buried in 1897. Describe the scene, including the contents of the capsule and the people who might have buried it.

95 **FOREIGN LANGUAGE**: Two people are having a conversation in a café, bar, or restaurant about something which has made them very angry or upset. Write some dialogue between the two people, incorporating four or five foreign-language words.

96 **TITLE**: *Yesterday's Call*
Use the title above to inspire a short story, dialogue, monologue, scene, or poem.

> "It is better to write a bad first draft than to write no first draft at all."
> —Will Shetterly

97 THANKSGIVING

Write down ten words you associate with Thanksgiving.

98 THANKSGIVING, PART TWO

Write a short paragraph about Thanksgiving using none of yesterday's words.

A RURAL LANDSCAPE

You're on a train traveling slowly through a rural landscape.
Describe what you see and how you feel.

100 VIEW FROM THE TOP

Imagine you are at the top of a very high tower or skyscraper. Write down what you can see and how you feel.

101 SURROUNDING SOUNDS

Listen very carefully to all the sounds that are surrounding you and write each of them down in detail.

102   LIPOGRAM "O"

A lipogram is a writing method whereby the author must avoid a certain letter, forcing a potentially unexpected take on, and challenging approach to, a subject.

Write a paragraph about crossing a passage of water by bridge or by boat, without using the letter "o."

---

103   LIPOGRAM "A"

Write a paragraph about an A-list celebrity without using the letter "a."

---

104   LIPOGRAM "B"

Write a paragraph about classic 1950s B-movies, without using the letter "b."

----

105   LIPOGRAM "T"

Write a paragraph about T-shirts, without using the letter "t."

INTENSIVE WEEK

Get your notebook and prepare to write five longer pieces.

106

DISTANT LOVE: Write the inner thoughts of somebody pining for a distant love.

107

COAST-TO-COAST: Write a short piece from the perspective of someone on a coast-to-coast journey by sleeper train, long-haul truck, or convertible Cadillac. Try controlling the pace by mirroring any action within the scene with sentence length. For example, short, sharp actions could be written in a few words: "Jenny sat back. She kicked her feet onto the dash. Her hand twitched. They were out of cigarettes." Whereas vivid and flowing passing scenery could be described using a long and flowing sentence, full of descriptive language and free of any stop/start punctuation: "Instead of nicotine she let the scent of the passing pine trees, fresh from the rainfall, flow through her open mouth and nose and deep into her lungs."

108

TORN: Think of a situation and write an internal dialogue for a character who is torn between being kind and selfless or selfish and hurtful.

109

TITLE: *The Blind Busker*
Write a short piece using the title *The Blind Busker* as your inspiration.

110

CARNIVAL: Write a short passage describing all the sights, smells, sounds, textures, and tastes of an old-style carnival.

> *"Be obscure clearly."*
> —E. B. White

111 FINDING WORDS

Look around you to find some words, any words. Try to find at least five words or even a sentence. This might be ingredients on the back of a cereal box or a newspaper headline. Write down the words or sentence and then follow on with your own passage, letting your writing wander in any direction.

112 HEIRLOOM

Write a short piece of dialogue between grandfather/grandmother and grandson/granddaughter, discussing a family heirloom.

113   TERRACOTTA SUNSET

Write down the colors of various natural materials and then use these material/color couplets to describe something else, such as "a terracotta-red sunset."

WHAT IF . . .?

A "What if . . .?" story scenario is a method for ideas generation. For example, "What if vampires invaded a small New England village?" This "What if . . .?" scenario became Stephen King's *Salem's Lot*, which was also made into a film by Quentin Tarantino (*From Dusk Til Dawn*). Write some "What if. . .?" story scenarios of your own.

What if . . .

What if . . .

What if . . .

What if . . .

HISTORICAL JUXTAPOSITION

Below are three famous historical events. Underneath each of them write a mundane, everyday occurrence that might have taken place on the same day, serving to juxtapose the historical events of the day.

The Great Fire of London begins in a bakery on Pudding Lane, September 2, 1666

V-J Day (the end of World War Two), September 2, 1945

Edmund Hillary and Tenzing Norgay reach the summit of Mount Everest, May 29, 1953

A GREAT ESCAPE

Write about a great escape, either real or imagined.

"I think that thing about the destruction of the world is there all the time, it's there every day when we look out the window."
—Peter Carey

DIALOGUE: COMPLAINT

Write a dialogue between two people talking on the phone where one person is making a complaint to the other.

---

118   VACATION SETTING

Describe your perfect vacation setting.

119   CITY SOBRIQUETS

Japan is known as the Land of the Rising Sun. Can you make up
five unique sobriquets for countries of the world?

INTENSIVE WEEK

Get your notebook and prepare to write five longer pieces.

120   **STREAM OF CONSCIOUSNESS:** Write the inner thoughts of a recently bankrupt businessperson contemplating the commercial world, sparked by an empty bottle of Coca-Cola tossed into the gutter. Write in a stream of consciousness style, with each thought flowing on from the last. Try to put yourself fully into the mind of the character and let your pen flow across the page.

121   **TITLE:** *I Remember Them*
What does the title *I Remember Them* mean to you? Does it spark ideas for a short story, monologue, poem, or perhaps something else?

122   **TIME CAPSULE, 1963:** A time capsule has been found following the digging up of ground at the end of the garden. It is discovered that the capsule was buried in 1963. Describe the scene, including the contents of the capsule and the people who might have buried it.

123   **TITLE:** *Out of the Darkness*
Use the title above to spark ideas for a passage of writing, long or short.

124   **FOUND ART:** Imagine a lost painting by a famous artist, worth millions, is found in an unusual place (by way of real-life example: a Van Gogh was once found covering a large hole in a chicken coop). Describe the circumstances of the discovery.

> "Get it down. Take chances. It may be bad, but it's the only way you can do anything really good."
> —William Faulkner

UNUSUAL ASSOCIATIONS

List five emotions (e.g. angry) and five facial expressions (e.g. pout).
Then match them up to form unusual associations, such as an
"angry pout."

emotion
e.g. sad

facial expression
wink

UNUSUAL ASSOCIATIONS, PART TWO

List five moods (e.g. pensive) and five body movements (e.g. stride).
Then match them up to form unusual associations, such as a
"pensive stride."

mood
e.g. grumpy

body movement
wave

AN UNEXPECTED DISCOVERY

Write about an unexpected discovery you make one day as you, or an imagined character, are walking down your street.

128 A PHOTOGRAPH

Describe a famous historical photograph, either from memory or from a copy placed in front of you.

129 YOUR FIRST TOOTH

Write about losing your first tooth.

130 THE MOON

Write down five to ten words you associate with the moon.

131 THE MOON, PART TWO

Write a short paragraph about the moon using none of yesterday's words.

132   THE SUN

Write down five to ten words you associate with the sun.

133   THE SUN, PART TWO

Write a short paragraph about the sun using none of yesterday's words.

INTENSIVE WEEK

Get your notebook and prepare to write five longer pieces.

134 **YOGI-ISMS:** Yogi Berra is a legendary baseball player for the New York Yankees. He inspired the cartoon character Yogi Bear and was famous for giving counterintuitive quotes during interviews, such as "Nobody goes there anymore—it's too overcrowded" and "It's like déjà vu all over again." Can you think of a "Yogi-ism?" And can you bring it into a passage of writing?

135 **LOST:** Write dialogue between two people who are lost in a city or in the country—whether it be they are physically lost and discussing how to find their way, or are simply lost in the conversation itself.

136 **SURVIVAL SITUATION:** Write a short piece, longer story, dialogue, or monologue from the perspective of a person or people who find themselves in a survival situation, whether they are castaways on a deserted island or in the heart of a hostage situation.

137 **TITLE:** *Gathering Dust*
Write a short piece, whether it be a short story, scene, dialogue, monologue, poem, or another form, using the title above.

138 **SIBLING RIVALRY:** Write a scene involving two brothers or sisters who have just found out they are vying for the same thing, whatever that may be; perhaps a job, a sporting competition, a love interest . . .

"My aim is to put down what I see and what I feel in the best and simplest way I can tell it."

—Ernest Hemingway

139 SUMMERTIME

Write about a vivid summertime memory, whether a memorable vacation, the last day at school, or a specific incident.

140 THE JOURNEY OF LIGHT

Write about the journey of light as it travels from the Sun to the Earth.

SETTINGS

Write a scene or passage based in one of the following settings: a coffee shop, a florist's, a restaurant, or a liquor store.

THE WRITING ON THE WALL

Under the following clichés write a new phrase which is less obvious and more original, but whereby the meaning is the same.

The writing on the wall (something clear and already understood)

Only time will tell (to become clear over time)

Scared out of my wits (to be too frightened)

A wise old owl (a wise old person)

DIFFERENT STROKES

Write down ten descriptive words each for angular and curved lines. Add facial expressions or emotions to each word to create unusual associations, such as a "jagged frown."

Angular line
e.g. jagged

Expression/emotion
frown

Curved line
e.g. undulating

Expression/emotion
sadness

THE WORLD BELOW

Imagine you are a bird, or in a plane looking out of the window at the world below. Describe what you feel and what you see.

CITIES OF THE WORLD

What word, words, or sentences do the following cities conjure up for you? If you don't know the city, then simply make it up:

Cape Town (South Africa)

Mexico City (Mexico)

Kuala Lumper (Malaysia)

Edinburgh (Scotland)

146 MARLON BRANDO'S CAP

Write a description of three stars or movie characters using their clothes to represent their character.

For example, "Marlon Brando's canvas biker cap in *The Wild One*, worn tilted; the left side fitted to his head, the right side teetering on the edge and bloating."

147 BABE RUTH'S PANTS

Write a description of three sports stars using their clothes to represent their character.

For example, "Babe Ruth's magnificent baseball pants, covered in earth and grit."

INTENSIVE WEEK

Get your notebook and prepare to write five longer pieces.

148 **WAKING UP:** Write a short story, scene, or plot outline using the "What if . . .?" scenario below.

What if when you wake up in the morning you see a different bed, a different room, and, when you open the curtains, a different city to when you fell asleep?

149 **A STRANGER:** Write a short story, scene, or plot outline using the "What if . . .?" scenario below.

What if a stranger was convinced you were their wife/husband and had hundreds of photos of you both together across decades as proof?

150 **TITLE:** *Changing Places*
Write a short story, dialogue, monologue, scene, or something different, based on the title above.

151 **PET DIALOGUE:** Write internal dialogue from the perspective of a pet dog (perhaps they are missing?).

152 **A HUMOROUS EXCHANGE:** Write an amusing exchange between two people who get talking in a bar. It comes to light that they both attended an interview for the same job that afternoon.

> "Love. Fall in love and stay in love. Write only what you love, and love what you write. The key word is love. You have to get up in the morning and write something you love, something to live for. "
>
> —Ray Bradbury

153 BABY HANDS

Describe a baby's hands and what they might be holding.

154 EATING AND DRINKING

Write down ten words associated with eating and drinking.

VERBAL TEXTURE

Below is a single line of dialogue. Rewrite the line using the voice of three different people with different accents and dialects.

"I can't make head nor tail of this instruction manual," he said, scratching his head. "I've a right mind to tear it into tiny little pieces, use it to light a fire, and then throw the damned television in the flames."

1.

2.

3.

156 ROCK CONCERTS

Write down five sounds you associate with rock concerts.

157 ROCK CONCERTS, PART TWO

Write a paragraph using some or all of the words from yesterday's prompt to describe a rock concert.

158 EXTREMES OF YOU

Looking into your own character traits and thinking how an extreme version of this trait might play out in a fictional character's personality can be a great source of inspiration. Write down some of the character traits you possess, however subtle they may be, which could be used to form a fictional character.

159 EXTREMES OF YOU: NAMES

Expanding upon yesterday's extremes-of-you character traits, write down three or four names of imagined characters who might personify these extremes of you.

160 EXTREMES OF YOU: SETTING

Expanding further upon yesterday's character names, describe the setting where these people might live out their lives.

161 EXTREMES OF YOU: DESIRES

Finally, describe their characteristics, their desires, what makes them tick, and the lives they lead.

INTENSIVE WEEK

Get your notebook and prepare to write five longer pieces.

162 **LEAVING THE RAT RACE:** Write a scene or dialogue involving an employee who goes about quitting their job in an unusual and unexpected way.

163 **TITLE:** *Leaving Forever*
Allow your imagination to flow using the title above as an initial spark to write a short story, dialogue, or internal monologue.

164 **TIME CAPSULE, 1704:** A time capsule has been found following the demolition of a shopping mall. It is discovered that it was buried in 1704. Describe the scene, including the contents of the capsule and the people who might have buried it.

165 **TEN-MINUTE FLOW:** Write continuously for ten minutes or longer, using the title *Never Too Far to Hear the Sea* as a trigger to start you off. Allow your mind to twist and turn and wander in any direction.

166 **AN UNUSUAL PERSPECTIVE:** Write about the city of Paris, or another city of your choice, from an unusual perspective, such as from the point of view of a 100-year-old woman.

"To have a great idea, have a lot of them."
—Thomas A. Edison

167 CELEBRATIONS

Write down ten words you might associate with celebrations.

168 A CARPENTER'S HANDS

Describe a carpenter's hands and what they might be holding.

MRS. MURPHY'S OVALTINE

Rewrite these strange but true song titles, replacing the subjects to create new, amusing scenarios or titles for a story.

"Who Put the Benzedrine in Mrs. Murphy's Ovaltine?" (Henry Gibson)

"The Day Ted Nugent Killed All the Animals" (Wally Pleasant)

"Ode to the Little Brown Shack Out Back" (Billy Edd Wheeler)

"Flushed from the Bathroom of Your Heart" (Johnny Cash)

A FACE

Describe all the elements of a face (hair, eyes, nose, lips, cheeks, ears) using unusual adjectives, descriptive sentences, and similes. For example, "lips like a red velvet chaise longue."

171 CHILDHOOD SHOES

Describe the first pair of shoes you remember wearing as a child. Where were they bought and who bought them for you? What do you remember about the detail of the shoes, and do they hold any lasting, meaningful memories?

AN UNEXPECTED MEETING

Write about an unexpected meeting with another person, either real or imagined. Where are you when it happens, and how does it make you feel?

"The true secret of happiness lies in taking a genuine interest in all the details of daily life."

—William Morris

EXTRATERRESTRIAL

Describe Earth to an extraterrestrial.

174 WHAT'S IN A TITLE?

Write down words you associate with the following book titles:

- *The Power and the Glory*, by Graham Greene
- *One Flew Over the Cuckoo's Nest*, by Ken Kesey
- *Whistle Down the Wind*, by Mary Hayley Bell

175 MUSICAL INSTRUMENTS

Write down ten words you associate with musical instruments and the sounds they make.

INTENSIVE WEEK

Get your notebook and prepare to write five longer pieces.

176   **CHARACTER BUILDING:** Write a simple, short sentence about a potential new fictional character, e.g. just their name, sex, age, and occupation. Rewrite the sentence three times, adding something new about their lives each time, to slowly build up a picture of the character.

177   **TEN-MINUTE FLOW:** Without stopping, and letting your instincts lead you, write for ten minutes or longer using the title *Getting Even* to start you off.

178   **CLAIMED BY WATER:** Write an apocalyptic image of the city of Venice, Italy (highly populated and built on 118 islands and a network of rising-level waterways), within a scene or short story set in a time before, during, or after the city has been claimed by water.

179   **HISTORICAL DIARY:** Write a diary entry for somebody who has experienced or witnessed a dramatic historical event or time, e.g. a girl writing about her father returning from the Vietnam War.

180   **PILOT AND COPILOT:** Write dialogue between a pilot and copilot mid-flight. The pilot is opening up about having a drinking problem. Add tension to the dialogue by having conflicting tones. For instance, the pilot is fractious and the copilot sensitive, or the pilot timid and the copilot angered at the potential danger to the plane and passengers.

> *"Logic will get you from A to B. Imagination will take you everywhere."*
> —*Albert Einstein*

181 CHILDHOOD TASTES

Write down five tastes that take you back to your childhood.

182 CHILDHOOD TASTES, PART TWO

Create a sentence or short paragraph using some or all of the words from yesterday's childhood tastes.

WINDING ROADS

Write continuously until you reach the end of the page, using any or all of the following words or phrases to trigger your thoughts:

- winding roads
- never in a month of Sundays
- butterflies

184   MORNING COFFEE

Describe the taste, smell, feel, and associations of an early morning coffee.

185   CLASHING COMBINATIONS

Write some unusual/clashing combinations of people and their actions or appearances. For example, "a homeless man wearing a donated tuxedo" or "a fireman striking a match to light a cigar."

186 TIME PORTAL

You, or an imagined character, are in the year AD 10,000. Where are you, how did you get there, and what do you see?

---

187 PUNGENT PLACES

Use the adjectives below to create descriptions of people, places, or things:

- pungent
- medicinal
- syrupy
- herby
- spicy
- acidic

188   SUNBEAMS MAY BE EXTRACTED

Using the unique and creative book titles below for inspiration, write down three potential titles for short stories, novels, poems, or whatever it is you may want to write.

- *Sunbeams May be Extracted from Cucumbers but the Process is Tedious,* by David Daggett
- *Dating for Under a Dollar,* by Blair Tolman
- *Somebody Else is on the Moon,* by George H. Leonard

---

189   ANIMAL SOUNDS

Write down five common animals and the sounds they make but avoid the obvious (e.g. cow/moo, dog/bark). Think of new and surprising ways to describe the sounds they make.

INTENSIVE WEEK

Get your notebook and prepare to write five longer pieces.

190   **TITLE:** *An Unopened Book*
Write a short piece in whatever form you choose using the above title to inspire you.

191   **PHONE DIALOGUE:** Write a dialogue between two people talking on the phone about an unusual incident they both witnessed the day before. How do they remember the details? Do they agree or disagree on what happened? How does each of them feel? How might dialogue on the phone differ from face-to-face dialogue?

192   **TITLE:** *The Greatest Ever*
Write a short story, dialogue, monologue, scene, or poem based on the title above.

193   **BACK STORY:** A woman has been arrested on suspicion of taking part in an armed robbery. Write a paragraph or two detailing her back story.

194   **POINTS OF VIEW:** Write a short scene with a third-person narrative, in which a fight breaks out in a hospital between an abusive, drunken man with an injury to his arm and hospital security. Rewrite the scene from the point of view of the two protagonists and an onlooker. You could either write the scene three times, each with a different point of view, or write a single scene with an interchange between the three points of view.

> "You can't depend on your eyes when your imagination is out of focus."
>
> —Mark Twain

195   BUILDING

Describe a famous building.

_____
_____
_____
_____
_____
_____
_____
_____
_____

196   CANDLES AND LAPTOPS

Take two objects, like a laptop and a candle, and write down any ways in which they are similar. For example, we might look into the screen of a laptop and into the flame of a candle. You could also think about the colors, textures, or uses of the objects.

_____
_____
_____
_____
_____
_____
_____
_____

THINGS TO ENJOY

Write about the things you enjoy most in life.

UNEXPECTED COMPARISONS

Take these common similes and make up new, unexpected comparisons.

As clear as mud

As clear as . . .

As solid as oak

As solid as . . .

As tough as old boots

As tough as . . .

As cunning as a fox

As cunning as . . .

NATURAL MATERIALS

Think of objects that might be made of the following natural materials and describe them in detail, perhaps also putting them into a context. For example, you could describe copper piping in detail and perhaps where it leads to through the bathroom floor and into the hidden basement.

- wool
- copper
- gold
- clay

AN ARID LANDSCAPE

You're traveling in a Conestoga wagon passing slowly through a flat, arid landscape. Describe what you see and how you feel.

IDIOSYNCRACY

Make a list of ten idiosyncrasies that could be used in a description of a person, such as "a man with a cigar permanently propped between his teeth."

202 SPORTING MOVEMENTS

Write down five examples of movements in sport. For example, "the swing of a golfer."

---

203 SPORTING MOVEMENTS, PART TWO

Taking yesterday's sports movements, create five sentences using adverbs to illustrate the sportsperson's character and movement. For instance, "The golfer swings his seven iron precisely, shaping a perfect arc through the air."

INTENSIVE WEEK

Get your notebook and prepare to write five longer pieces.

204

FIVE WHYS: Five Whys is a method you can use to help plot development. Start by writing a simple action that a character might do and a setting, e.g. "A man is sitting on a stool in a bar and lights up a cigarette." Ask the question "Why?" and give the answer "Because . . ." For example, why (1) is he sitting on a stool in a bar, lighting up a cigarette? Because he is stressed. Why (2) is he stressed? Because he has just lost five million dollars. Why (3) . . . etc. By the time you have asked five whys you will have expanded upon the character(s), the settings, any problems and conflicts, and developed plot.

205

TITLE: *Unbroken*
Creating a context to the title *Unbroken*, write a short story, dialogue, monologue, or scene.

206

HEAVEN AND HELL: What would heaven, hell, and purgatory be like if you were to visit?

207

TITLE: *The Tree on the Hill*
Where is the tree on the hill? Is it real or metaphorical? Let the title inspire you to write a short piece in whatever form you wish.

208

A BOAT'S STORY: Write a short piece from the perspective of a boat (e.g. a fishing boat, a whaling ship, a tug boat, etc.), describing the world surrounding it and the things it has encountered and witnessed across the years.

> "A rock pile ceases to be a rock pile the moment a single man contemplates it, bearing within him the image of a cathedral."
> —Antoine de Saint-Exupéry

209 FAMOUS PAINTING

Describe a famous painting, either from memory or from a copy placed in front of you (or from real life if you are in an art gallery, or have a famous painting on your wall!).

210 ANIMAL DISASSOCIATION

Describe an animal, including three words you would not normally associate with that animal.

AUTHOR SIMILES

Create your own similes in place of the authors' similes below.

" . . . impressions poured in upon her of those two men, and to follow her thought was like following a voice which speaks too quickly to be taken down by one's pencil . . ."—*To the Lighthouse*, by Virginia Woolf

. . . impressions poured in upon her of those two men, and to follow her thought was like . . .

_____

_____

_____

"Some starlings had alighted on a wire overhead in perfect progression like a piece of knotted string fallen slantwise."
—*Suttree*, by Cormac McCarthy

Some starlings had alighted on a wire overhead in perfect progression like . . .

_____

_____

_____

"The process of cleaning had so shocked the fabric that it was now broken on the creases, papery and crumbling in his hand like the wing of a dead butterfly."—*My Life as a Fake*, by Peter Carey

The process of cleaning had so shocked the fabric that it was now broken on the creases, papery and crumbling in his hand like . . .

_____

_____

_____

212   TRANSPORT NOSTALGIA

Describe an old car, push bike, motorcycle, train, boat, or another mode of transportation, writing with a sense of nostalgia.

213   BIGGEST FEAR

Describe your biggest fear. Or make one up for an imagined character.

214   DIALOGUE WITH THE FUTURE

Write dialogue for a brief exchange with someone from the near or distant future.

215   AD **100,000**

You, or an imagined character, are in the year AD 100,000. Where are you, how did you get there, and what do you see?

216   SIGHT

Describe the following using words relating to sight:

- a bonfire
- the sea
- a cityscape

---

217   COLLOQUIALISMS

Write down a few words and sentences using slang words, colloquialisms, and dialect.

INTENSIVE WEEK

Get your notebook and prepare to write five longer pieces.

218 **A DRAMATIC PROPOSAL:** Write about a dramatic proposal and how the answer plays out. This might be an elaborate wedding proposal with a yes or no answer, or an illegal business proposal, or something else.

219 **CREATING CONFLICT:** Create conflict to develop plot. Write a premise for a story, e.g. a woman is looking for her estranged mother. Write something that might turn the premise into a conflict. For example, her mother is in a witness-protection program having become embroiled with the Mafia and does not want to be found. The resolution of the conflict can lead to the development of the plot.

220 **TITLE:** *Unchosen Paths*
Use the title above as a central theme to a short story.

221 **MULTIPLE NARRATIVES:** Reframe the following line in the first person, the second person, and the third person, adding in greater detail to the scene: "A man walks into a pool hall, orders a whiskey and ice at the bar, and demands to speak to the owner."

222 **EVACUATED:** Write a short story, scene, or plot outline using the "What if . . .?" scenario:

What if your town was evacuated for classified reasons and you were forced to live on a giant commune?

> "To invent, you need a good imagination and a pile of junk."
> —Thomas A. Edison

223   LOST KEYS

Write a brief passage involving a character who has lost the keys to their home but must urgently enter the property.

----

224   WORD PROGRESSION

Underneath the words "enchanting" and "elephant" write a continuous list of words, with each word having an association with the previous one, until you reach the thick line. Use the first two and last two words in the list to create a sentence underneath the line.

enchanting　　　　　　　　　　**elephant**

═══

SETTING A SCENE WITH SONG

Songs are a great way to define mood or set a scene. Write down the titles of two or three of your favorite songs. Incorporate each song title into the setting of a scene.

For example, "The sentimental sounds of Louis Armstrong's 'What a Wonderful World' danced inside Eddie's head as he strolled along the sidewalk towards the café where Lisa was waiting."

ONLY A MATTER OF TIME

Rewrite the clichés below to create a phrase that is less obvious, more interesting and dynamic, but which offers the same meaning.

It's only a matter of time (to happen sooner or later)

All's fair in love and war (to do anything in order to claim somebody's love)

More haste, less speed (it's quicker to do things efficiently rather than in a rush)

Too many cooks spoil the broth (too much input from too many people gives poor results)

WORD CONSTRAINT: MOVIES

Pick three of your favorite movie titles. Count the number of letters in the title and write a short description or review of the movie using this number of words.

e.g. *Life is Beautiful* = 15 letters
Description/Review = 15 words

A PHOTOGRAPH

Write about a photograph that has sentimental value for you, either from memory or with one placed in front of you. Or create a fictional photograph, imagining why it is so special.

"The visionary starts with a clean sheet of paper, and reimagines the world."
—Malcolm Gladwell

INTO THE AIRPORT

Starting with the sentence "The plane flew into the airport" write continuously, without stopping, until you reach the end of the page.

The plane flew into the airport . . .

230 PORTMANTEAUS

Make up some portmanteaus, whereby two words are combined to form a new word that has two related meanings, such as "smog" (an instance of weather that looks like both smoke and fog). Or "eleventeen" (a mature eleven-year-old).

231 PORTMANTEAUS, PART TWO

Put yesterday's portmanteaus, whether your own or the examples given, into context. This could be dialogue, the setting of a scene, a character description, or something else.

INTENSIVE WEEK

Get your notebook and prepare to write five longer pieces.

232 **A UNIQUE VOICE:** Write a monologue for a character with a disorder of some sort, such as Tourette's syndrome or obsessive compulsive disorder. They could be talking about their disorder or something else. How might this come out through their voice?

233 **FIVE WHYS:** Write a line describing a character performing an action in a setting (see prompt 204) and ask the question "Why?" followed by the answer "Because..." five times for scene and plot development.

234 **NEW WORDS:** Grab a dictionary and find four words you have never previously heard of and use them to write a passage describing a journey through a town or city.

235 **TEN-MINUTE FLOW:** Write with minor deliberation for ten minutes or longer, using the title *Electric* to set you on your way. Let your thoughts flow and see where your stream of consciousness takes you.

236 **TEXTURES:** Describe the feel of the following:
- a leather jacket
- a rock
- a stream
- a waterfall
- gnarly old wood

"It is perfectly okay to write garbage—as long as you edit brilliantly."

—C. J. Cherryh

237   TICKER TAPE

Write down five objects that might be found on the streets of a city following a ticker-tape parade.

238   TICKER TAPE, PART TWO

Expand upon yesterday's found objects, describing them in detail.

A PROWLING TANK

Think of both an animal and a vehicle. Describe each of them using words that would normally describe the motions of the other.

For example, "The tank prowled the village roads."
"The panther stuttered across the plain, dragging its injured leg."

240 LETTER

Write a short letter to a movie star or character from history.

_____

_____

_____

_____

_____

_____

_____

_____

_____

241 LETTER REPLY

Write a reply to yesterday's letter from the movie star or historical figure.

_____

_____

_____

_____

_____

_____

_____

_____

_____

242 SILENCE

Write down all the words you associate with silence.

_____

_____

_____

_____

_____

_____

_____

_____

243 STORY SETTINGS

Write down five settings for a potential story.

_____

_____

_____

_____

_____

_____

_____

_____

244 A POSTCARD FROM HERE

Write a "postcard" to a distant friend, relative, or someone imagined, the "holiday" location being wherever you are right now.

245 SIGHT

Describe the following using words relating to sight:

- clouds
- a rusted automobile
- a waterfall

INTENSIVE WEEK

Get your notebook and prepare to write five longer pieces.

246   **HITCHHIKER:** Write two pieces of internal dialogue from the perspective of two people experiencing the same scene but with clashing interpretations. The scene consists of a hitchhiker and a driver who have been driving and talking for two hours but have now fallen silent.

247   **TEN-MINUTE FLOW:** Let your pen flow across the page for ten minutes or longer, using the title *The Great Indoors* as an initial spark.

248   **TITLE:** *Lost and Found*
Take inspiration from the title above to inform a passage of writing.

249   **A HUMOROUS EPISODE:** Write a comical encounter between an employee and their boss.

250   **FOUR SEASONS:** Write four descriptions of a single building, street, or country landscape, reflecting the changes that occur as a result of the four seasons.

> "If you have other things in your life—family, friends, good productive day work—these can interact with your writing and the sum will be all the richer."
> —David Brin

251 SOUNDS OF CHILDHOOD

Write down five sounds that take you back to your childhood.

252 SOUNDS OF CHILDHOOD, PART TWO

Create a sentence or short paragraph using some or all of the words from yesterday's childhood sounds.

253

PAINTING CHARACTERS

Think of, or find an image of, a famous painting that includes people within the scene, such as *Nighthawks* by Edward Hopper (1942). Pick one or two people and write down who they are, or who you imagine them to be, and what they are thinking.

POLAR WINDS

Use similes to describe and expand upon the effects of the extreme weather conditions below. For instance, "The polar winds forced their way through his fur-lined hood and formed ice crystals on his beard like metal shards to a magnet."

- polar winds
- El Niño
- pyroclastic flow

CITIES OF THE WORLD

For each of the cities below write a word, words, or sentences that you associate with them.

Vienna (Austria)

Toronto (Canada)

Cairo (Egypt)

Moscow (Russia)

A MYSTERIOUS BAG

You, or an imagined character, find a mysterious bag in the attic. What does it look like, what is inside, and how did it get there?

DESIRES

"When I used to teach creative writing, I would tell the students to make their characters want something right away—even if it's only a glass of water. Characters paralyzed by the meaninglessness of modern life still have to drink water from time to time."
—Kurt Vonnegut

Write down five desires that you, or an imagined character, are compelled to pursue, whether they are big, grandiose plans, unusual goals, or simply reaching for a glass of water.

THE FIVE SENSES

Try to get as many of the five senses of sight, sound, smell, taste, and touch/feel into a single sentence as you can. In the following line from *As I Lay Dying,* William Faulkner has feel, taste, sight, and smell:

"Warmish-cool, with a faint taste like the hot July wind in cedar trees smells."

LITERAL MEANINGS

Write a list of five objects. Next to these objects write their literal meaning, to create interesting alternatives.

Object	Literal meaning
e.g. automobile	people carrier

INTENSIVE WEEK

Get your notebook and prepare to write five longer pieces.

260   **SYNESTHESIA:** Write about a character (in a scene, a character profile, or a dialogue with another person) who suffers from synesthesia, where they see tastes and smells as colors.

261   **THE OPERA HOUSE:** Write about somebody watching a symphony orchestra in an opera house. Write about the emotions and memories the music and surroundings evoke.

262   **TITLE:** *The Letter*
What is in the letter? Or is it a letter of the alphabet? What significance does it have to a character or characters? Write a short story using the title *The Letter* for inspiration.

263   **DRIFTWOOD:** Imagine you are on a bridge over a river watching a piece of driftwood float gently past you and away. Describe this image and the journey of the driftwood as it passes down the river, wherever the journey might end.

264   **TEN-MINUTE FLOW:** Using the title *A Rusted Boat* write in a stream of consciousness, letting your thoughts come to the page with speed and flow. Precision of sentences and structure are unimportant. What is important is to tap into your unconscious thoughts and into a well of inspiration.

"Words are a lens to focus one's mind."
—Ayn Rand

265 WHAT'S IN A TITLE?

Write down words you associate with the following book, movie, and song titles:

- *One Hundred Years of Solitude,* by Gabriel García Márquez
- *The African Queen*
- "Time to Say Goodbye," by Andrea Bocelli

266 HOT-AIR BALLOON

Write about a trip, real or imagined, in a hot-air balloon.

HISTORICAL JUXTAPOSITION

Write a mundane, everyday event that might have occurred on the same day as the historical events below.

George Washington inaugurated as first US president, April 30, 1789

Nelson Mandela released from imprisonment, February 11, 1990

Indian Ocean earthquake and tsunami, December 26, 2004

268 WALKING

Write down ten alternative words for walking.

269 WALKING, PART TWO

Write sentences using some of yesterday's alternative words for walking.

270 YOUR TOWN

Describe your town, city, or village, or wherever it is that you live.

---

271 FIREWORKS

Describe the colors, sounds, and smells of fireworks in the sky.

272 FRESH SNOW

Imagine someone is seeing a snowy scene for the very first time. How do they describe it? How does it make them feel?

273 NATURE BUILDING

Using only words associated with nature, describe a city or building.

INTENSIVE WEEK

Get your notebook and prepare to write five longer pieces.

274   **FAIRGROUND ATTRACTION:** Write two short pieces about a person, or people, visiting a fairground attraction. Write the first account describing a time of fun and laughter. Then write the second account imagining the setting to be sinister and dark.

275   **TEN-MINUTE FLOW:** Write for ten minutes or longer, using the title *Final Steps* as an initial spark. Stretch your writing muscles and see where your thoughts take you.

276   **THE CAVE:** Write about an imagined character spending a day and night in a cave. What are the circumstances and what does the darkness do to their thoughts and perceptions?

277   **TITLE:** *It Never Ended*
What does the "it" refer to in the title above? Create an intriguing short story or episode to unravel the mystery.

278   **FRESH FALL LEAVES:** Write down words, sentences, or similes to describe the sounds made by the following:
- stepping on fresh fall leaves
- construction work
- a building being demolished
- a tree being cut down
- walking in the snow

"Writing is its own reward."
—Henry Miller

279 THE WEIRD AND THE WONDERFUL

Below are some weird and wonderful book titles. Using these as inspiration, write down three potential titles for short stories, novels, poems, or whatever it is you may want to write.

- *Anybody Can Be Cool . . . But Awesome Takes Practice*, by Lorraine Peterson
- *There's a Wocket in My Pocket!,* by Dr. Seuss
- *What to Say When You Talk to Yourself,* by Shad Helmstetter

---

---

280 EVERGREEN FOREST

Imagine you are in an evergreen forest. Describe the sights, smells, and sounds of your surroundings.

SECRETS AND OBSESSIONS

Write down a brief description of some fictional characters and either their secrets or obsessions.

UNEXPECTED COMPARISONS

Take these common similes and make up new, unexpected comparisons.

They fought like cats and dogs

They fought like . . .

_____

_____

_____

She slept like a log

She slept like . . .

_____

_____

It fits like a glove

It fits like . . .

_____

_____

_____

As sweet as a nut

As sweet as . . .

_____

_____

_____

FIERY PEOPLE/PLACES/THINGS

Use the adjectives below to create some descriptions of people, places, or things:

- ashy
- smokey
- fiery

- warming
- alarming
- charred

A LETTER

Write a short letter to a real or imagined friend or relative, either telling them about a momentous incident, musing generally about life, or something else completely.

A REPLY

Write a reply to yesterday's letter from your real or imagined friend or relative, capturing their unique voice and including any specific words and turns of phrase they may use.

286 DANCE

Write down five examples of movements in dance. For example, "the pirouette of a ballerina."

287 DANCE, PART TWO

Taking yesterday's dance movements, create sentences using adverbs to illustrate the character and movement. For instance, "The ballerina pirouettes effortlessly."

INTENSIVE WEEK

Get your notebook and prepare to write five longer pieces.

288   **HIDDEN AND UNDISCOVERED:** Use the following scenario to create a character profile or profiles of the person or people involved, thinking about what their back story might be, why they find themselves where they are, and what might be their goal/mission.
A person or group is trekking across the Siberian plains in order to reach and cross the Bering Strait, a seasonal bridge of ice between Russia and Alaska, before the ice melts. They have little money and must remain hidden and undiscovered.

289   **HOSTILE ENCOUNTERS:** Following on from yesterday's Siberian-plains scenario, write a scene or scenes using the following dramatic events that the person/group experiences:
- The stalking of an East Siberian brown bear in order to make extra-warm clothing from its pelt
- An encounter with locals in a remote, hostile vodka bar
- An attack by an Amur leopard

290   **ANY DIRECTION:** Continue the Siberian story, now adding dialogue.

291   **TITLE:** *Soul Harbor*
Write a short story, dialogue, monologue, scene, poem, or another form of writing using the title above to inspire you.

292   **VITRIOL:** Imagine an altercation with another person. Write dialogue showing a real sense of anger and vitriol.

> "Every secret of a writer's soul, every experience of his life, every quality of his mind, is written large in his works."
> —Virginia Woolf

293 THE NIGHT SKY

Write down five to ten words you associate with the night sky.

294 THE NIGHT SKY, PART TWO

Write a short paragraph about the night sky using none of yesterday's words.

TASTES

Describe the taste of the following:

the sea air

ripe strawberries

traffic fumes

crusty bread

a pungent perfume

296 NOT TASTY

Use the four elements of taste below as adjectives for words not associated with taste.

- bitter
- sweet
- salty
- sour

---

297 THE PERFECT MEAL

Describe your perfect meal, including a description of the food, the location, the ambience, and company. What would it be like if it were the last meal of an imagined character on death row?

298 ACRONYMS

Using a person's name (real or imagined), treat it as an acronym and come up with the nonabbreviated version, which relates directly to that person. For example, a possible obituary for the unique, dark-humored, satirical sci-fi author, K.u.r.t.V.o.n.n.e.g.u.t.:

Kilgore "Useless Riter" Trout. Vignettes of nonsensical nuttiness; effortless greatness—until toast.

299 EYES

Write ten varying descriptions of eyes.

300   VOCAL SOUNDS

List three vocal sounds. Next to each of these write how the sound affects your hearing and how you feel. For example, "mellow-soothes." Then use these words to write one or two sentences, such as, "His mellow voice would soothe me as I listened to his stories."

vocal sound   **effect on hearing**

301   SHOPPING MALL

Write down all the sights and sounds you might experience in a shopping mall.

INTENSIVE WEEK

Get your notebook and prepare to write five longer pieces.

302 **COMMUNITY CONFLICT:** Write a scene, dialogue, or story outline involving someone who is experiencing conflict within their community, such as racial or class conflict. Who are they, what might the conflict be, how are they affected, and how do they overcome it?

303 **TITLE:** *Message Never Sent*
Use the title above to take your writing in any direction you wish; in any style, in any form.

304 **DERELICT HOTEL:** Write a description of a derelict building (such as an old school or a rundown hotel, including all of the five senses to bring life to the subject.

305 **TEN-MINUTE FLOW:** Initiate a ten-minute free flow using the title *The Phone Call* as a trigger. Try to add an element of structure as you write to guide your free flow into a coherent story, monologue, scene, or episode, without losing the sense of fluidity in your writing.

306 **FATHERLY ADVICE:** Write a piece of dialogue between a father, who is offering advice, and his son.

"If it sounds like writing, I rewrite it. Or, if proper usage gets in the way, it may have to go. I can't allow what we learned in English composition to disrupt the sound and rhythm of the narrative."

—Elmore Leonard

307 ZEUGMAS

A zeugma uses a single verb to form two parts of a sentence. For example, "She broke his door and his heart." Write some zeugmas of your own.

308 THE JUNGLE

Write down all the sights and noises you might see and hear in a jungle.

CITIES OF THE WORLD

What thoughts, ideas, and feelings are conjured up when you think about the following cities of the world?

San Francisco (United States of America)

Casablanca (Morocco)

Berlin (Germany)

Madrid (Spain)

CITY SOBRIQUETS

Below are a list of sobriquets for cities across the world. Write alternatives that you, or an imagined character, might feel are more appropriate to your experience or perception of the city. For instance, Ushuaia, Argentina (The End of the World) might feel more like "The New Beginning."

London, United Kingdom (The Old Smoke)

Cairo, Egypt (The Paris of the Nile)

Beijing, China (The Forbidden City)

Budapest, Hungary (The Pearl of the Danube)

Jaipur, India (The Pink City)

Seattle, United Sates of America (The Emerald City)

Lima, Peru (The City of Kings)

A DIAMOND IN THE ROUGH

Make up some new phrases to replace the clichés below to offer a more creative alternative while maintaining the meaning.

A diamond in the rough (one having exceptional qualities or potential but lacking refinement or polish)

Lasted an eternity (to last for a very long time)

All's well that ends well (a happy ending reduces the severity of problems that occur along the way)

Many hands make light work (a job can be made easier with the help of more people)

HISTORICAL JUXTAPOSITION

Juxtapose the three historical events below with a seemingly mundane, everyday event that might have occurred on the same day.

The Wall Street Crash, October 29, 1929

Neil Armstrong lands on the moon, July 21, 1969

The fall of the Berlin Wall, November 9, 1989

PAINTING CHARACTERS: A CITYSCAPE

Think of, or find an image of, a famous painting of a cityscape or urban setting. Write down what you, or an imagined character, might be thinking if the scene were real and you, or they, were standing within it.

314 ICEBERG

Think of an object, a building, or a place. Write details that can be
seen and also what might be unseen, such as how it makes you
feel and how it affects the senses.

e.g. a book
Seen: fusty worn pages, a faded dust jacket
Unseen: sadness, pleasure, an author stooped over a typewriter

Seen

_____

Unseen

_____

315 A PLACE TO IMAGINE

Think about a place you have always wanted to visit and write
about how you imagine it to be.

_____

INTENSIVE WEEK

Get your notebook and prepare to write five longer pieces.

316   **FIRST DATE:** Write internal dialogue from the perspective of a couple on a first date. Both have excused themselves to their respective restrooms and are looking in the mirror, touching up their hair or makeup, and revealing their thoughts about the other. Do their opinions match or conflict?

317   **TEN-MINUTE FLOW:** Taking the title *Unlocked*, begin with an initial plan for a story or dialogue and where it might go: a beginning, middle, and end. Once you have an idea of character, story, and setting (no matter how basic or complex this might be) let your pen flow and write with speed to inject an essence of raw fluidity to the piece.

318   **MARKET STALL:** Write a description of a market stall including all of the five senses to bring life to the setting.

319   **TITLE:** *Last Chance Saloon*
Is last chance saloon a place, a feeling, a situation, or something else? How might answers to these questions emerge in a piece of writing?

320   **A DESERTED VILLAGE:** You, or an imagined character, are walking through a deserted village. What buildings do you see? Who once lived and worked here? Why is it now deserted?

> "Let the world burn through you. Throw the prism light, white hot, on paper."
> — Ray Bradbury

321   STORMY SKY

Write down five to ten words you associate with a stormy night.

322   STORMY SKY, PART TWO

Write a short paragraph about a stormy night using none of yesterday's words.

OXYGEN ICE CREAM

List three things you couldn't live without, and three things that you love but could live without. Mix them up to form new ideas, which are potentially jarring and unexpected:

e.g. Couldn't live without: oxygen
Could live without: ice cream
Forms: oxygen ice cream
New idea: "The cookie-dough ice cream she sold was like sweet oxygen; the entire neighborhood could not live without it."

Couldn't live without:

_____

_____

_____

Could live without:

_____

_____

_____

New ideas:

_____

_____

_____

_____

_____

_____

_____

_____

THE BEACH

Write a description of a beach, including all of the five senses to bring life to the setting.

BULL IN A CHINA SHOP

Write continuously until you reach the end of the page, using any or all of the following words or phrases to trigger your thoughts:

- like a bull in a china shop
- cafe latté
- traffic jam

ONE-DOLLAR BILL

Write in as much detail as possible about a note or coin of currency, such as a one-dollar bill, either from memory or from looking at one placed in front of you.

> "Write while the heat is in you. . . . The writer who postpones the recording of his thoughts uses an iron which has cooled to burn a hole with."
> —Henry David Thoreau

NYLON STOCKINGS

Think of objects that might be produced using the following man-made materials and describe them in detail, perhaps also putting them into a context. For example, describe nylon stockings, placing them in the context of Second-World-War deprivations:

- polyester
- plastic
- glass
- nylon

328 INDOOR SOUNDS

List five sounds that indoor objects make. Then list the object that is usually associated with the sound, and then an object that is less obviously associated.

Sound word	Normal association	Less obvious
e.g. creaks	door	sofa

329 OUTDOOR SOUNDS

List five types of weather, followed by the sounds they make, both loud and soft.

Weather	Loud	Soft
e.g. wind	howls	whispers

INTENSIVE WEEK

Get your notebook and prepare to write five longer pieces.

330   **WONDERFUL THINGS:** Taking Howard Carter's famous phrase when he first looked upon the site of Tutankhamen's tomb, "I see wonderful things," imagine where you might be looking to see wonderful things, and what you see.

331   **FIVE SENSES OF CHARACTER:** Write a passage including a description of an imagined character, or someone you know, using all of the five senses to bring life to the character.

332   **TITLE:** *Through Hell and Rainfall*
Use the title above to write a piece in the form of your choosing.

333   **TIME CAPSULE, 1932:** A time capsule has been found following the repair of electrical cables outside an office block. It is discovered that the capsule was buried in 1932. Describe the scene, including the contents of the capsule and the people who might have buried it.

334   **THE MUSEUM:** Write a scene or dialogue between three people who find themselves trapped in a museum after lockup and begin to encounter unforeseen problems.

> *"Don't wait for moods. You accomplish nothing if you do that. Your mind must know it has got to get down to work."*
> —Pearl S. Buck

335 BODYBUILDERS IN TUTUS

In a similar vein to the weird and wonderful book titles below write down some jarring images (e.g. bodybuilders in tutus) or actions (e.g. teaching physics to your dog):

- *This Is the Best Book I've Ever Written, and It Still Sucks (This Isn't Really My Best Book)*, by Jarod Kintz
- *Bodybuilders in Tutus*, by Philipp Lomboy
- *How to Teach Physics to Your Dog*, by Chad Orzel

336 ELDERLY HANDS

Describe an elderly person's hands and what they might be holding.

337 BOOK LIST

Write a list of the last five books you have read. Describe each one in only three words.

338 BOOK LIST, PART TWO

Take the words from yesterday's exercise and use them to write a short description either of your day yesterday or your week.

339 MARDI GRAS

Write down all the words you associate with Mardi Gras and street parades.

340 RAINFALL

Write down ten words you associate with rainfall.

341 WAR . . .

Describe or define war in a few concise sentences.

342 . . . AND PEACE

Describe or define peace in a few concise sentences.

343   CHILDHOOD PLACES

Write down five places that take you back to your childhood.

344   CHILDHOOD PLACES, PART TWO

Create a sentence or short paragraph using some or all of the words from yesterday's childhood places.

INTENSIVE WEEK

Get your notebook and prepare to write five longer pieces.

345

FOUR CORNERS: Write a short piece using the following scenario: A couple stop in their car at Four Corners, where Arizona, New Mexico, Utah, and Colorado meet. Which direction do they take and why? How do they decide and why are they unsure which direction to go?

346

A STRONG VOICE: Write a short piece of internal dialogue for a character who is looking out of the window and contemplating how they came to be in the place they find themselves. Decide first of all where the character originates and write with fragmented words and incorrect grammar to create a strong colloquial voice.

347

THE SIDEWALK: Imagine you are standing on the sidewalk of a large town or city. Describe what you can see, hear, smell, taste, and feel.

348

TEN-MINUTE FLOW: Let your pen flow continuously for ten minutes or longer, using the title *Rise and Fall* as an initial spark. The results may inform a longer piece of writing, a character, or a specific scene. You can mine for ideas within the free flow of thoughts.

349

INHERITANCE: Think of something you have inherited. Describe it in detail, including any emotions you feel and its history.

"You must have chaos within you to give birth to a dancing star."

—Friedrich Nietzsche

350

OUTDOOR SOUNDS

List five sounds that outdoor objects make. Then list the object that is usually associated with the sound and then an object that is less obviously associated.

Sound word	**Normal association**	**Less obvious**
e.g. honk	automobile horn	sports air horn

351

SPORTS STADIUM

Describe the sights, sounds, and smells of a huge indoor or outdoor sports stadium, both when full of fans and when empty.

SHELTER

Describe the following places of residence and shelter and the people who live and rest in them:

- igloos
- soup kitchens
- winnebagos
- barges

AUTHOR SIMILES

Create your own similes in place of the authors' similes below.

"Her face was quiet and a curious look was in her eyes, eyes like the timeless eyes of a statue."—*The Grapes of Wrath*, by John Steinbeck
Her face was quiet and a curious look was in her eyes, eyes like . . .

_____

_____

"The ride was actually over in six and a half minutes, and I had no choice but to hobble like an off-balance giraffe on my one flat, one four-inch heel arrangement."—*The Devil Wears Prada*, by Lauren Weisberger
The ride was actually over in six and a half minutes, and I had no choice but to hobble like . . .

_____

_____

"All at once he sprang into jerky agitation, like one of those flat wooden figures that are worked by a string."—*Lord Jim*, by Joseph Conrad
All at once he sprang into jerky agitation, like . . .

_____

_____

"All sorts of pleasant things happened about that time, for the new friendship flourished like grass in spring."—*Little Women*, by Louisa May Alcott
All sorts of pleasant things happened about that time, for the new friendship flourished like . . .

_____

_____

WORD CONSTRAINT: SONGS

Pick three of your favorite song titles. Count the number of letters in the title and write a short description or review of the song using this number of words.

e.g. "On Silent Wings" = 13 letters
Description/review = 13 words

EVERY CLOUD

Create some alternative phrases to the clichés below that are less obvious, more interesting and dynamic, while offering the same meaning.

Every cloud has a silver lining (problems have a positive aspect)

Lost track of time (to stop paying attention to time)

Time heals all wounds (pain and misery passes over time)

As meek as a lamb (a person who is overly weak and humble)

A DESOLATE LANDSCAPE

You're in a limousine cruising through a desolate, industrial
landscape. Describe what you see and how you feel.

357 | TEXTURE

Add a layer or two of detail to the things listed below to add texture. For example, "a factory" becomes "a disused chemical factory."

- fairground
- mansion
- trailer park
- coffee shop

358 | FLYING THROUGH CLOUDS

Describe the sight of an airplane going through a cloud, either from the perspective of being inside the plane or looking at it from the ground.

INTENSIVE WEEK

Get your notebook and prepare to write five longer pieces.

359

TITLE: *Broken*
Compose a piece of writing in whatever form you are inspired to write using the title above, whether it be a short or long piece, reality or fiction, dialogue, or first-person narrative.

360

UNUSUAL PERSPECTIVE: Write about a city from an unusual perspective, such as from the point of view of a subway driver.

361

OBJECT FREE FLOW: Look around you to find an object, like a pen or a photo. Describe the object and continue to write for ten minutes or longer. Let your thoughts flow from one to the next without much, if any, deliberation. Do not worry too much about spelling and grammar—the key is to stretch your writing muscles and see where your thoughts take you.

362

THE BOXER: A boxer is knocked down in a fight, either an illegal bout in a disused abattoir or a huge fan-filled stadium, and is trying to make the count. Write about the action from the point of view of the boxer, his opponent, and a worried loved one.

363

TIME CAPSULE, 1984: A time capsule has been found following the digging up of turf in a school's grounds. It is discovered that the capsule was buried in 1984. Describe the scene, including the contents of the capsule and the people who might have buried it.

"Belief and reader absorption come in the details: An overturned tricycle in the gutter of an abandoned neighborhood can stand for everything."

—Stephen King

364 SKYLINE

Imagine you are looking out over a city's skyline. Describe what you see and how you feel for each of the four seasons.

Winter _____

_____

Spring _____

_____

Summer _____

_____

Fall _____

_____

_____

365 LAKESIDE

Imagine you are looking upon a lake. Describe what you see and how you feel for each of the four seasons.

Winter _____

_____

Spring _____

_____

Summer _____

_____

Fall _____

_____

_____

NOTES